THE FACTS OF LIFE

Faith, Action, Change, Truth and Service

Guy Jazzy Rainey

THE FACTS OF LIFE
FAITH, ACTION, CHANGE, TRUTH AND SERVICE

iUniverse books may be ordered through booksellers or by contacting:

iUniverse
1663 Liberty Drive
Bloomington, IN 47403
www.iuniverse.com
1-800-Authors (1-800-288-4677)

ISBN: 978-1-4917-7115-0 (sc)
ISBN: 978-1-4917-7116-7 (e)

Library of Congress Control Number: 2015910197

Print information available on the last page.

iUniverse rev. date: 06/26/2015

CONTENTS

All that I am, or hope to be, I owe to my angel mother.

—Abraham Lincoln

I would like to dedicate this book to three women who were an integral part of my childhood and adolescence. Their guidance and love gave me all that I would need to become the man I am today. The first of these is my mother, Ella Mae Green-Rainey; her love and strength kept me moving in the right direction. As you will soon find out, that was not an easy task. Speaking of her strength, many of our close friends and family referred to her as Sarge (short for sergeant); however, her military-type strength would prove critical to my upbringing in the mean streets of Harlem. Mom, I want to thank you for providing me with all the tools I needed to succeed; you often speak of how proud you are of me, and I want to say how very proud I am of you. May peace be upon you. I miss you like crazy.

Second, I'd like to thank my aunt Louise Rainey Haywood (Aunt Weez) for teaching me to be proud of my Rainey heritage and to never give up on my dreams. I miss you so much. I wish you could see me now, because I am the fruit of your life's work.

Last but not least, I'd like to thank my oldest sister, Marie Diane Green, for showing me that the spirit of God's love is endless and that his kindness will always be with me. You showed me how to be fearless in the face of fear and, no matter what, to face all challenges with the spirit of a conqueror. I miss you calling me Key-Key.

The love and power of these three women allowed me to imagine that I was a boy prince and that I could conquer the world. Thank you! Thank You! Thank you! Love you always and forever.

John and Ella's Baby Boy

I would like to send a special dedication to my friends of thirty-five years. To Omar Chandler (Chandler Spencer)—I remember the days of doing shows at local clubs for cab-fare home. I remember when Leon Brill, the owner of Broadway International, told you to change your name to Omar. You thought he was crazy until I told you no one in show business uses his or her real name. We are going to miss you deeply. RIP. I love you, man. R&B music will never be the same without you.

I'd like to also dedicate this book to my best friend, Andre Grey. I remember when we used to jam in my room and my mother would yell at us to turn the music down. I miss those days, and I miss you too. RIP, my homie. We made hip-hop smile.

And to my brothers, Walter and Curtis—my love for you guys will never change. RIP.

Mr. Gregory Batson, DTM, PDG, you were my mentor and friend. I will miss you dearly. From the time I became part of Toastmasters, you took me under your wing and pushed me into a new comfort zone, and for that I thank you. May peace be upon you.

To my father-in-law, Alvan Allen Sr. You will be deeply missed. You took me under your wing and taught me the simple joys of fatherhood. I appreciate and thank you for that. I love the fact that my children got the chance to be loved by you. It's going to be strange not to be able to call you about how to fix a leaky pipe or how to replace a roof shingle. Maya Angelou once said, "People won't remember what you said or what you did, but they will always remember how you made them feel." And you, Dad, always made us feel loved. May peace be upon you. Say hi to my mother for me. With love, your son-in-law, Jazzy.

FOREWORD

I found Guy Jazzy Rainey's book *The FACTS of Life* very compelling. I have known Mr. Rainey for approximately three years. We are members of the Freeport-Hempstead chapter of Toastmasters International. I have heard him deliver powerful speeches on many aspects of his life in person at our club meetings. Now he shares them with his readers.

Mr. Rainey grew up in Harlem and had three tragedies back to back, which would have taken most men down. His mother was diagnosed with bronchitis, his aunt died from cancer, and his wife discovered a lump in her left breast. On top of that, when the economy took a turn for the worse, he had to file for bankruptcy. One week before he turned fifty, his best friend was murdered.

After all these events, he decided to keep the faith, write his story, and bless the reader with this powerful book of how he found the strength to keep going. We can all gain insights to combat life's struggles.

The title is an acronym for Faith, Action, Change, Truth, and Service.

I am impressed that Mr. Rainey read many inspirational books from great thinkers such as Napoleon Hill, Zig Ziglar, Joel Osteen, Maya Angelou, Dr. Wayne Dyer, and Mahatma Gandhi.

He taught me to find answers to life's problems by reading about the men and women who have climbed up the rough side of the mountain. The book is powerful because he shares his personal stories. Two stories that struck me were how he learned the word *entrepreneur* and his love for the music industry.

Mr. Rainey turned to his faith before he made any big move. Here are a few highlights from his chapters:

- In his "Faith" chapter he says, "Faith takes over and leaves fear behind to achieve goals."
- In his chapter called "Action," he reminds us that his parents instilled in him the notion of hard work. He reminds us that Maya Angelou said, "Nothing will work unless you do." This has been a part of his life from childhood to today.
- In the chapter "Change," he reminds us to change our *attitudes* toward what is happening to us.
- In "Truth"—I can relate to staying in the moment and being truthful to my beliefs, even when the going gets rough.
- Mr. Rainey demonstrates a unique perspective in the chapter "Service" when he tells us that the best way to serve others is to serve yourself and take care of yourself first.

With these five principles the reader will be able to examine his or her life and find areas of growth and ways to lead a more fruitful and productive life.

Other scholars he quoted come from a variety of backgrounds: Abraham Lincoln, Norman Vincent Peale, Harriet Tubman, Oprah Winfrey, Barack Obama, Craig Valentine, Les Brown, and finally Rev. Dr. Martin Luther King Jr.

I am confident that the reader will be inspired. No matter what obstacles you face, you can overcome them with Faith, Action, Change, Truth, and Service.

Dr. Darrell W. Pone

Acknowledgments

First of all, I would like to thank the Most High Almighty God and our ancestors for giving me the will and strength to write this book.

Next, I would like to thank my wife, Debbie, for being my rock through good times and bad. We have been together for a quarter of a century, and I'm looking forward to the next quarter of a century with you. I love you like a fat kid loves cake.

I want to thank my children, Simone, Jasmine, Guya, and Nigeria (a.k.a. the Girls), for believing in me. Daddy couldn't have done it without your support. And I thank my granddaughter, Nyla. I love you girls with all my heart.

I'd like to thank my best buddies: Anthony Chisolm (author of *The Adventures of ZIGGY*), for making me man up and write, and for believing in my dream—thank you, my brotha. Thank you, Big Bob Moss, for mentoring me when I needed it the most. And Kevin Williams, my brother from another mother—it was our tough Harlem upbringing that made us strong. I love you, man. Derek Bass, even when I was sad, you always kept me laughing. Edwardo and Diana Jose, thank you for keeping true love alive.

I'd like to thank my mentees: Edward, Glen, Jerel, Jeral, Kwesi, Malik, Manny, Kyle, Anthony, Steven, and Jermaine. You guys are the inspiration behind writing this book. My hope for you guys is that you take the baton and run with the tools and knowledge I've passed on to you; pay it forward.

To my little sis, Chenise Djomambo—from the first day we started hanging out, friends called you the female version of me. Stay strong, sis. To my brother Earl and my sister Yvonne—I love you guys deeply. Blood is thicker than water. My Detroit family, Motown will always be my second home.

I would like to give a special thanks to the three men who mentored me when this boy really needed a man in his life. First to Isaac Roberts—you were my spiritual guide and big brother; you are one of the reasons why this book comes to life. Thank you for your love and guidance.

Second, thank God for Mr. Byron, my eighth-grade teacher. I hated going to school on the Lower East Side (LES) of Manhattan. I couldn't understand why my mother would send me down there in the first place, but I understand now; it was God's divine order.

Last but not least is Coach Ford, my high school JV basketball coach. You showed me how to be a leader and told me to always lead for the right reasons and not to follow for the wrong reasons. Thank you, Coach: it's my motto.

Because of these three men, my life is full of promise, and I have plenty of love to pay it forward. Thank you.

Shout out to my nieces, Kendekka and Fatima, for helping me see my vision when sometimes my vision was blurry. To my editor, Melissa Scott—you are a lifesaver. To my Toastmaster mentors, Dr. Darrell Pone and Dr. Gloria Nixon-Pone—simply thank you. Good looking out Coach Lee Street. My LegalShield mentor, Mr. Troy Randall, thanks for the wake-up call. To Afrika Bambaataa & the Universal Zulu Nation, for having my back when no one else had my back.

Special shout out to my Green and Rainey family. Too many to mention—you all know who you are, and you know I love you all.

God bless you all.

INTRODUCTION

A friend asked me what inspired me to write this book about overcoming life's challenges instead of about the music business. That's a good question! First of all, let me tell you the reason I've chosen to write about this subject. When I was a little boy growing up in Harlem, USA, things happened in my life that truly defined who I am today. I'm the youngest of six children. After my father passed away, my mother worked two jobs to make ends meet. Being the baby of the family had its perks. My siblings would often shield me from some of the hardships they were going through. Even though I have seen lots of turmoil in my life, I've also experience lots of joy. When I was a teen, my mother went back to school and later started her own daycare. As I got older, I learned that all the principles I was taught by my mother, aunt, and older sister would guide me to overcome life's challenges. They taught me that through *faith* all things are possible. Taking *action* would help me move forward in life. They showed me that *change* is good and to stand in my *truth*, because my word is bond. The most important lessons I learned from these three women are that family is where your strength comes from and to always be of service. Those lessons and five principles are my suit of armor that helped me grow and survive in the music business, which at times was a scary place to be in.

For more than twenty years the music business was my life. I started out as a DJ and then became a club promoter and then a record executive. I've also worked at record stores, recording studios, and radio stations. Music was my life. After marrying the love of my life and moving to Long Island, my life took a different turn when my sister Diane and my brother Curtis passed away; my hunger for a greater spiritual calling started to grow. Losing them made me feel empty inside, and the music business wasn't doing it for me anymore. After the birth of our daughters Guya and Nigeria, I started my new life as a nine-to-five, punch-in, and punch-out union civil servant. Three years after the death of my oldest brother, Walter, my mother, who was diagnosed with COPD and congestive heart failure, was told she had six months to a year to live. At the end of 2012, Aunt Mildred from Detroit, Michigan, passed away after a long battle with cancer.

In 2013, my wife found a lump in her left breast. After multiple tests, the results came back positive for breast cancer. She had to have a mastectomy plus a lumpectomy on her right breast. Now I had to take care of the two most important women in my life, my mother and wife. When I thought things couldn't get any worse, my real estate business took a nosedive, and we had to file for bankruptcy. Then one week before my fiftieth birthday, my best friend of thirty-five years was murdered in his home. I started to go into a deep depression; I felt like life was beating me down and winning.

One day I was watching a video on YouTube by Lisa Nichols. As she was talking about her days as a high school swimmer, she said she would come in last every time—as she put it, "dead last." She went on to tell about how she wanted to give up. Her grandmother sat her down and told her, "A quitter never wins, and a winner never quits." At her next swim meet, she kept repeating to herself, over and over, what her grandmother told her: "A quitter never wins, and a winner never quits." Not only did she win; she also became the all-state swimming champion that year. Watching that video gave me a glimmer of hope.

After watching her video, I watched another video by motivational speaker Ian J. Humphrey called *It's Not About the Knockdown*. He starts out with, "Boom! Down goes Muhammad Ali." He told the story about how the boxing champ was knocked down for the first time in his life; he said to himself, "This is no place for a champ." Then he got up and beat his opponent. At that moment I knew I had to get up and fight back.

When I made that conscious decision, God spoke to me and said, "It's time to write about what you are going through."

I'd started to doubt my ability to write. I didn't know exactly how to say what I was feeling. That month I went to a leadership workshop by 1209 Affairs, featuring George C. Frazier, author of *Success Runs in Our Race*, and Dr. Dennis Kimbro, author of *The Wealth Choice*.

Before Mr. Frazier spoke and introduced Dr. Kimbro, everyone was networking with each other and passing around business cards. I noticed Dr. Kimbro standing on the side. I wanted to go up to him and tell him all the great things I'd learned from his online classes from Clark Atlanta University, but doubt kicked in again and fear grabbed hold of me. As I debated whether or not I should go over and talk to him, I remembered something he said in one of his videos. He told a student that he could achieve the same success he had. He said, "The only difference between you and I is that I have more classroom hours than you."

At that moment I got up from my seat and walked over to introduce myself. He seemed delighted to meet me and genuinely happy to know that I'd read his book, *Think and Grow Rich: A Black Choice*. I told him I'd used his book to teach my mentees about the importance of being more enterprising in today's world.

Talking to Dr. Kimbro that day made me realize that all things happen for a reason. The people you meet will be either lessons or blessings in your life. The next day in the shower, it hit me like a ton of bricks, as my mother would put it. That really meant God was sending you a message and you better start listening. In that state of peace and stillness, God spoke to me and said, "You can do this!" Instead of having fear, have Faith. Instead of being abused, take Action. Instead of committing crime, make a Change. Instead of being in turmoil, stand in your Truth. Instead of being selfish, be of Service.

In my life journey, I've learned you always have choices. Some of us, because of our upbringing, tend to look at things from a negative perspective instead of a positive one.

The energy you use to think and act negatively is the exact same energy that can be used for positive thoughts and actions. You may have been raised in a negative climate, but you were not born to be negative.

This book is written in five chapters. Each chapter is designed to help you work through the ups and downs of life's challenges. Because I had someone in my life to help me overcome the chaos that surrounded me growing up, I feel it's my duty to pass on the lessons I've learned along the way.

These five principles—Faith, Action, Change, Truth, Service—are the principles all successful people live by. They are not the only principles successful people live by, but these five are part of their principle philosophies. I once read a sign that said, "A lion that doesn't hunt for its food is just a house cat." I've put that sign on my wall at home, and I look at it every day. It's my reminder to always take full responsibility for my actions. My hope for you is that you will keep this book with you on your journey and pass the lessons on to a loved one.

Have a blessed day, and pay it forward.

FAITH

Cherish your visions and your dreams, as they are
the children of your soul, the blueprints of your
ultimate achievements.

—Napoleon Hill

Definition of Faith

*Allegiance to duty or a person; loyalty; fidelity to one's promises; sincerity
of intentions; belief and trust in and loyalty to God; belief in the
traditional doctrines of a religion; firm belief in something for which
there is no proof; complete trust.*

As a child I was always a big dreamer. Thinking big was a way
of life for me.

So many of my friends would laugh at me and say, "There he
goes again, talking that talk." Most of my friends thought I was
crazy to think up some of the ideas I came up with.

But in spite of all the criticism and naysayers, through faith I
created my own space in life. I truly believe we can all achieve our
highest goals by creating visions of possibility.

Talk show host and network owner Oprah Winfrey, the world's
best-known inspirer, said, "Create the highest, grandest vision
possible for your life, because you become what you believe."

1

On my twelfth birthday, my mother took my niece and I to a Broadway musical called *The Wiz*. This play is still one of my favorites of all time. After we saw the play, my mother bought me the soundtrack.

When I got home, I put the album on right away and called my two best friends, Kevin and Karl, over to hear the incredible music from this incredible production. Before they got to my apartment, I had already created my own version of the play, and I wanted them to participate in my new adventure as a director and playwright. So in my room we made *The Wiz—My Way*.

I always felt like I could create and produce with the best of them. What I know for sure is that every successful creator and producer of any product or business has to have faith in God and believe in their talents and their abilities to make it happen. Your faith is the number-one source for your success. It is the reason you keep going.

Faith is the reason most people strive to win. Without faith, most of us seem to give up on our goals and dreams. Growing up in Harlem, I remember seeing people who were addicted to drugs and alcohol, and I wondered to myself, *How did they get that way?*

I remember when my oldest brother, Walter, was addicted to drugs and how it was destroying him and our family. One day my brother Earl and I came home from school to find Walter slumped over on the bathroom floor with a needle stuck in his arm, barely breathing. Earl ran downstairs to our neighbor's apartment; she was a nurse. She rushed upstairs and revived Walter and saved his life.

That was one of the scariest days of my young life. The craziest and saddest thing about that situation was that it wasn't the first time he overdosed—and that wasn't the first time our neighbor had to save his life. On that day I'd told myself, *I will never do drugs.* And to this day, I've never done any.

Back then I thought my family had some type of dark cloud over us, because my other brother Curtis, who fought in the Vietnam War, was also addicted to drugs. So many things occur in our daily lives that we can sometimes feel that the world is against us, so we look to outside forces to make things better (e.g., drugs, alcohol, and risky behavior). The fact is, those things will never make it better.

Even though my brother Walter had gone through living hell with his drug addiction, he finally overcame his addiction a year later by getting help and taking responsibility for our ailing grandmother, who was suffering from kidney failure.

I was so proud to see my oldest brother face his fears and ask my mother for help so he could move to South Carolina and help my grandparents with their quality of life. Before my brother Walter passed away, we often talked about the changes he made in his life for the sake of his family. Your "why" will keep you motivated when things are at their worst.

And when you feel lost and defeated, it will be your "why" that will help give you the strength and encouragement to go on. Napoleon Hill, the great author of *Think and Grow Rich,* said, "Before success comes in any man's life, he's sure to meet with much temporary defeat, and, perhaps some failures. When defeat overtakes a man, the easiest and the most logical thing to do is to quit. That's exactly what the majority of men do."

In my life, I've met so much temporary defeat, and one might wonder why I have not given up yet. I've always told my children that keeping my faith in God, myself, and the people who can help me reach my goals in life is what keeps me moving straight ahead toward my dreams.

There will be times in your life when you'll feel like you are the only one on earth with a problem as big as yours. But the truth is, there is always someone who can empathize with you, someone who is going through the same exact situation you are now going through. There was a time in my life when I thought my prayers were going unanswered. But when I dig down deep in my soul for the answer to my troubles, that's when God always reveals the solution.

In words of the great Albert Einstein, "That deep emotional conviction of the presence of a superior reasoning power, which is revealed in the incomprehensible universe, forms my idea of God." One thing that I know for sure is that faith is the key to any achievement in life. If you want to achieve your goals, faith must take over, and you must leave your fears behind.

As my mentor Les Brown, motivational speaker, simply puts it, "Too many of us are not living our dreams because we are living our fears."

When you can share your dreams with others (in my case my wife and children), it encourages them to reach for greater goals.

All things start with a dream and then an idea. Faith will be your first step toward your dreams. The great Reverend Dr. Martin Luther King Jr. once said, "Faith is taking the first step even when you don't see the whole staircase."

When times are at their hardest, keep your faith stronger than ever. Winston Churchill said, "If you're going through hell, keep going."

Sometimes things can get a little overwhelming. One day my wife and I were talking about how the past year was especially tough on us. She felt like every time we took two steps forward, we seemed to take three steps back.

At times, life will lead you to question your faith in God and ask the question, Lord, why me? I told my wife, "I look at life as if it's a bow and I'm the arrow. It sometimes pulls me back, but when I let go and let God, then the bow (life) releases the arrow (me), and I shoot straight ahead to hit my target, and the target is always my goal."

Minister and televangelist Joel Osteen said it best: "God didn't make a mistake when He made you. You need to see yourself as God sees you."

At times when my faith is challenged, I find a quiet place to meditate and have a deep conversation with God.

During my most trying times, I began to thank God for giving me the strength to carry on. Showing gratitude for the good in your life is where you begin to find the solutions to your problems. If you take one step toward God, he will take two steps toward you. In the words of Mother Teresa, "We need to find God, and he cannot be found in noise and restlessness. God is the friend of silence. See how nature—trees, flowers, grass—grows in silence; see the stars, the moon and the sun, how they move in silence ... We need silence to be able to touch souls."

Your faith is the prelude to all your actions. Without faith, you may be like that broken clock on the wall. You may be right twice a day, but you'll never move. The reason we act like that broken clock and don't move forward in our lives is because we entertain the negative talk in our heads, which brings his friends (fear, doubt, and uncertainty) along.

When you entertain negative thoughts and allow the naysayers to take control of your life, you will never achieve your dreams.

There are three things you can do to help you move forward when you are feeling like life is beating you down:

1. You must forgive yourself and know that you are good enough.
2. Know that only you can complete you.
3. Take a chance on life, and live it to the fullest.

This is what I know for sure: your faith and your fears cannot coexist. The first lady of civil rights and the mother of the freedom movement, Rosa Parks, once said, "I have learned over the years that when one's mind is made up, this diminishes fear; knowing what must be done does away with fear."

In the summer before I entered the third grade, my family and I went on a bus trip to upstate New York. On the bus ride coming home, I felt really sick to my stomach and started to become feverish. When we got home from the bus trip, my mother took my temperature and gave me some medicine for my upset stomach.

Nothing my mother gave me that night seemed to work, so she took me to the hospital to see what was wrong with me.

At the hospital, the doctor ran some tests to see what was causing my fever and why nothing would stay down. After running a few tests, the doctor told my mother I had a cold; he gave me cold medicine and sent me home.

At home, I felt worse than I felt the day before, and my fever rose higher and higher. My mother started to worry, because I couldn't walk or talk, and the pain was overwhelming. The only sounds coming from me were moans and groans as a stream of tears ran down my face. My mother took me to a different hospital.

Because I couldn't walk, my mother had to carry me on her back down four flights of stairs, from our apartment building.

When we got to the hospital, the doctor took me in right away and ran more tests on me. He told my mother he thought I had meningitis; they would have to start a spinal tap on me immediately.

My whole family was in a panic. My grandmother told my mother not to allow them to perform the spinal tap because it would paralyze me.

My entire family came together to pray and show support. That was when my mother's faith was really being challenged, and fear was standing at attention. I can remember being in pain and being scared, wondering why this was happening to me. I was so afraid. I wouldn't let anyone hold me down and allow the doctor to inject me with the longest needle I'd ever seen in my life.

About six nurses tried to hold me down, but I was not having it. I was going into the third grade, but I felt as strong as an ox. If you had seen the size of that needle you would understand. They got an orderly who was the size of NFL football great Mean Joe Greene to hold me down. He looked at me and said, "Are we going to do this the easy way or the hard way?"

I remember curling up like a cat and putting all my faith into God that day. I was in no way going to give that big orderly any trouble. When he grabbed me, his big hands around my arms and legs, I felt at peace and safe in his care.

William Shakespeare once said, "Now, God be praised, that to believing souls gives light in darkness, comfort in despair."

My test came back positive for meningitis, and I had to be quarantined. That was the loneliest feeling in the world. When my family came to visit me, they had to put on hospital scrubs, masks, and gloves.

Even though I was only in the third grade, my relationship with God came to light that year. I spent the whole summer in the hospital and had to learn how to walk all over again.

I got two more spinal taps before I was put in a room with other children.

I started getting better and making new friends in the hospital. I would wheelchair race with other kids up and down the halls of the children's ward. But going home was the best day of my young life.

I was still weak, and I didn't start school until late October that year. School was a little tough on me because I had to play catch-up. But I thanked God for giving me the strength to survive such an ordeal.

The doctors told my mother if she had waited one more day before taking me to the hospital, I would have died.

To this day, I still have scar tissue on the right side of my brain, which causes severe migraines as a result of the meningitis. But when I look back on that time in my life, I understand there's a purpose for everything under the sun.

I know keeping God first in your life will give you the peace of mind you need. In Matthew 17:20, Scripture says, "Because you have so little faith. Truly I tell you, if you have faith like a grain of a mustard seed, you can say to this mountain, 'Move from here to there,' and it will move. Nothing will be impossible for you."

What I notice today in most people I come across is they are not suffering from a lack of faith—they have no faith. Sometimes we look at all the craziness that's going on around us and focus only on the wrong that goes on in the world, which is easy. When you turn on the news or pick up a newspaper, all you see or read about is turmoil and despair.

You can easily get caught up in the external circumstances of living, which appears to have a limited nature; you forget that you are unlimited because you're connected to a God-source. Mahalia Jackson, an American gospel singer possessing a powerful contralto voice, is referred to as "the Queen of Gospel." Mahalia said, "Faith and prayer are the vitamins of the soul; man cannot live in health without them."

Remember: faith and fear are direct opposites, and faith is the driving force behind overcoming all adversities. Faith is your foundation toward action. Through God, all things are possible.

It's Possible (All Things Are Possible.)

From the time I was a little boy growing up in Harlem, my sister Diane would always tell me, "Your dreams can always come true."

I remember my sister taking my niece and me to the movies to see what would become my favorite movie, *Willie Wonka and the Chocolate Factory*. In the movie, the main character, Charlie, dreamed of winning a free trip to a magical candy factory with his grandpa Joe. But because his family was very poor and couldn't afford some of the simple things the other kids could afford, it seemed impossible. One day Charlie found money on the street, and he bought two candy bars, hoping one had the golden ticket.

Charlie's mother and Grandpa Joe would always tell him all his dreams could come true if he kept the faith and that great things would come his way. Before he opened his candy bar, he closed his eyes and prayed very hard that this time would be the time something great would happen. When he opened the second candy bar wrapper, he beheld a golden ticket!

Mary McLeod Bethune was an American educator and civil rights leader best known for starting a school for African-American students in Daytona Beach, Florida; it eventually became Bethune-Cookman College. She said, "Without faith, nothing is possible. With it, nothing is impossible."

The one thing you have to hold on to is your faith. God will see you through any problem that may come your way. There's an affirmation my wife and I state daily: "Through God, all things are possible."

Just because things seem to go wrong for you at times doesn't mean your story is written in stone or that your life will always roll in a downward spiral. Sometimes it takes life's defeats to teach you the proper lessons needed for achieving success. British Army officer T. E. Lawrence, also known as Lawrence of Arabia, said, "All men dream, but not equally. Those who dream by night in the dusty recesses of their minds, wake in the day to find that it was vanity:

but the dreamers of the day are dangerous men, for they may act on their dreams with open eyes, to make them possible."

When you dream that impossible dream with no limits, the universe starts to open up to you with endless streams of possibilities. Under no circumstance should you ever give up. I know at times you feel like calling it quits, but you have to keep on pushing and pushing for greatness.

Dwight Lyman Moody, also known as D. L. Moody, was an American evangelist and publisher who founded the Moody Church, Northfield School, and Mount Hermon School in Massachusetts and the Moody Bible Institute and Moody Publishers; with his words I concur: "Faith makes all things possible ... love makes all things easy."

I recall that in my tenth grade English class, I was telling my teacher about all the projects I was involved with outside of school. He said to me, "Guy, do you know what they call people like you? Entrepreneurs! Have you ever heard that word before? I want you and the class to look it up."

My classmates were angry that they had to do more classwork than expected, but I was fascinated with the word I had never heard before. As the teacher wrote the word *entrepreneur* on the board, the smartest kid in the class read the meaning out loud. I said to my teacher, "I like that word! That's what I'm going to call myself from now on."

Everyone has a defining moment in their life, and that day in English class was mine.

Since that day, I've owned a carpet-cleaning business, a recording company, an event-planning business, a recording studio, a production company, a real estate company, and a few Multi-Level Marketing (MLM) companies. In between starting and trying to maintain those businesses over the last thirty years, I've also worked my fair share of many other jobs, just to pay the bills.

Dreaming big is the only way I know how to dream. I did well for myself in the music businesses. But when I took on other business ventures, I made so many mistakes and faced many temporary defeats, which sometimes made me wonder if I was cut out for it. But through the grace of God, I always moved forward with my dreams and passions. In his book, Think and Grow Rich, Napoleon Hill says, "There is one quality which one must possess to win, and that is definiteness of purpose, the knowledge of what one wants, and a burning desire to possess it."

I remember when I used to play games in my neighborhood, like stickball and flies up. Those games were spin-off street games of baseball. Back then, I wasn't very good at baseball or its spin-off games.

Then one summer, my mother sent me to a sports camp for baseball and basketball. That summer, learning the fundamentals of baseball from the pros and coaches gave me a new perspective on my full potential for playing baseball. In fact, the next school year I tried out for the team and made first-string center fielder.

I'm telling this story not to impress you but to impress upon you that hard work and opportunity are the pathways to success. In the words of motivational speaker Tony Robbins, "What we can or cannot do, what we consider possible or impossible, is rarely a function of our true capability. It is more likely a function of our beliefs about who we are."

If you keep dreaming that dream and work on it, the world of possibility will come your way. In the words of Zig Ziglar, "It's not where you start—it's where you finish that counts."

We tend to dwell on the negative things in our lives instead of the good things. The mind then becomes obsessed with negative things, with the judgments, guilt, and uncertainty that cause anxiety. Such thoughts about the future tend to send us into a tailspin that we think we cannot solve at the present time.

But when you put your mind on the level of highest creativity, the possibility for reaching your goals are endless. Filmmaker and actor Tyler Perry once said, "You may not be at your goal yet, but what you need to know is that with each step you get closer. Take some time to stop and thank God for where you are, stop focusing so hard on the finish line and enjoy the race."

Give the universe your best, and in return you will receive the best that life has to offer. Stay true to who you are, and keep God first. Learn to love yourself, and be the best you as God intended you to be.

Sometimes I keep my fears to myself, so I can share my inspirations with others.

You have to find your inner peace through forgiveness. If you are having difficulty letting go of anger and resentment toward someone that has brought harm to you in the past, it will just hold you back from being the true and great you that God meant for you to be. Advocate for righteousness, and stay in God's favor.

Bishop T. D. Jakes once said, "Not forgiving someone of your past that done you harm, is like drinking poison and hoping the other person dies." Let go and let God, for you, not the other person. Own your power, and stand in your truth. Pay it forward, and find your new earth filled with happiness.

As you face the daily challenges that life puts in front of you, it is your job to take each challenge head-on and affirm that nothing will get in your way.

Use your strength to help guide you on your journey through life, and thank God for that strength.

This is your time to break away from the herd and declare your independence. Put your faith in God, and believe in your inner strength.

This is the day you will turn all encounters into opportunities.

Be passionate about life, and give thanks to God for the opportunity to greet each new day. Every morning you will thank God for the opportunity to explore your greatness.

Your zeal for living includes helping others and being of service. Stay enthusiastic about your spiritual practice, and study so that you may learn and grow for the evolution of your soul.

From this day forward, your alarm clock will be known as your opportunity clock.

Take responsibility for your actions, and stand in your truth. Tire executive Harvey Firestone once said, "You get the best out of others when you get the best out of yourself." So put your best foot forward.

Hold on to your happiness, no matter what happens in your life journey. The law of the universe is what goes around comes around. So go forward and spread joy, and joy will come back to you.

Praise God that every waking moment is a great moment.

> Now faith is the substance of things hoped for, the evidence of things not seen.
>
> —Hebrews 11:1

Keep the faith!

Notes

ACTION

Nothing ever comes to one that is worth having,
except as a result of hard work.
                                          —Booker T. Washington

Definition of Action

*The bringing about of an alteration by force or through a natural
agency, the manner or method of performing.*

As a little boy I thought of chores as punishments. My mother
used to get upset with my brother Earl and I when we would try to
leave the house without making up our beds and doing our daily
chores. I always felt like the bed would just get messy again anyway
once I climbed back into it that night. But to my mother, keeping
a clean room was one of my duties, and doing daily chores was the
beginning of a good work ethic.

When you are young and sometimes look at things from an "I
don't care" perspective, your parents or guardians have to sometimes
set you straight about the type of path you are taking. I come from
what you might call a "worker bee" kind of family, or working-class
people. My parents and grandparents were all hardworking people
and believed that working hard and playing hard meant all would
be right with the world. The great poet Dr. Maya Angelou said it
simply and plainly: "Nothing will work unless you do."

I remember when at the age of sixteen I started my career in the music business as an intern at the world-famous nightclub Harlem World. Back then interns were not called "interns;" we were called "gofers." In the very early eighties of hip-hop music, you had to be quick on your feet or you'd lose your spot to someone who wanted it more than you. One day I bought a new Adidas jacket and put the name of the nightclub on the back of my jacket. The managers were so impressed with what I did, they brought me over to the owner to show him what I'd done on my own. Later that year, management gave me more responsibilities in the club, which led me to ask if I could start up my own dance school at the nightclub in the summer months. The owner and managers gave me the green light. With my friends Larry Love, Jerome, and Dwight, we started the Harlem World Dance Troupe. I tell this story because when opportunity knocks on your door, just taking the simple action of answering it will open many doors for you.

Dr. Norman Vincent Peale, the author of *The Power of Positive Thinking,* says, "Action is a great restorer and builder of confidence. Inaction is not only the result, but the cause, of fear. Perhaps the action you take will be successful; perhaps different action or adjustments will have to follow. But any action is better than no action at all."

Before I started my career as a motivational speaker, taking immediate action on a project was always the plan. Following through on that project was sometimes a different story. When working for someone else, I was known as a man of action. But when it came to working for me, I would sometimes procrastinate and move on to a new idea when things got a little bit tough. Instead of moving forward on a project, I would move on to the next easy thing, fearing that I might be making a big mistake. But I've learned through the years that making mistakes is just growth; your mistakes will be your greatest teachers. Henry J. Kaiser was an American industrialist who became known as the father of modern

American shipbuilding. He said, "When your work speaks for itself, don't interrupt."

I was recently talking to an old friend of mine, and we got on the subject of putting words into action. She asked me, "Why can't men say what they mean and mean what they say?" I told her words are an emotional tool people use to communicate. We have all (at one time or another) said to someone, or to ourselves, things like, "I'm going to do this," "I'm going to do that," or, "I'll get around to it." All of us have at one time said things that had no actions behind them. Our words indicate what we think, and our thoughts create our worlds. In order for things to move forward in life, we have to start putting some verbs in our sentences and follow through with vigor. Vince Lombardi, one of the NFL's greatest coaches, once said, "The only place success comes before work is in the dictionary."

Dale Carnegie was an American writer and lecturer. He was also the developer of famous courses in self-improvement, salesmanship, corporate training, public speaking, and interpersonal skills. He said, "One of the most tragic things I know about human nature is that all of us tend to put off living. We are all dreaming of some magical rose garden over the horizon instead of enjoying the roses that are blooming outside our windows today."

When it comes to decision making, simply work toward your goals, make the wise choice to put God's gift into action; stay true to who you really are. God gives us all gifts, talents, and abilities. And it's up to us to tap into them with creativity, manifest them, and share the manifestations with the world. My mentor, Toastmaster's 1999 world champion of public speaking, Craig Valentine, once told me: "The Beijing Olympics is coming up, right? Have you ever seen track and field? Do you know what the real tragedy is, if we take the track and field metaphor? Whether it comes to using your unique gifts or selling your guide or writing a book or doing whatever you want to do, living your dream, most people live their lives on 'get set,' right?"

When you take immediate action on your dreams with passion and determination, nothing can hold you back. Most people give up on their dreams by the time they reach the age of thirty-five. But in reality, thirty-five is the perfect age to take action on beginning your new life. My life coach and mentor Bob Proctor said, "The only way to start life with a new paradigm is to get rid of the old paradigm."

Pablo Picasso was a Spanish painter, sculptor, printmaker, ceramicist, and stage designer who spent most of his adult life in France. He said it like a true artist: "Action is the foundational key to all success."

I recently watched a TED Talk; the speaker said, "Most people who talk about what they are going to do with their life plans are more likely not to complete their life goals." He said when you continually talk about what you are going to do, you trick your brain into thinking you have already been working on your idea. When you write down your ideas and set a timeline and a deadline to your ideas, that's when you can take charge of your thoughts and actions, and at that time you will see things start to come together for you and your dreams. There is an old saying: action speaks louder than words. There's also a new saying in conjunction with that old saying: don't talk about it, *be* about it.

I've learned that instead of focusing on a problem, you should concentrate on the solution. Eighty percent of people today live in a life box that I call "abusive reality." Some people would rather stay in a situation that is abusive to the goodwill of their souls instead of changing. Plato once said, "The curse of me and my nation is that we always think things can be bettered by immediate action of some sort, any sort rather than no sort."

In order to make a change in your life, you must move out of your comfort zone and do the things you only dream about doing. Give life a chance on that burning desire that keeps you up all night and has you tossing and turning. You can only grow when you are willing to feel awkward and uncomfortable about trying something new. God's grace will see you through.

Work On Your Dreams (Dream Big and Often)

When my mother was a little girl she dreamed of being an actress and becoming a big movie star like Shirley Temple. But my grandmother had other plans for my mother: for her to become a secretary. In my mother's days of growing up, the only roles in Hollywood for African-Americans were portraying domestic characters. My grandmother was a domestic worker, and the last thing she wanted to see was her daughter portraying her lifestyle on the big screen. Not realizing what she was doing, she helped kill my mother's dream of being an actress by telling her only the lighter-skinned black girls got the best parts in the school plays and that she was wasting her time auditioning for the lead. Most parents think saving their kids from future heartache and pain is being a good parent. But the truth is, they're really killing dreams. Famed poet Langston Hughes said, "I Iold fast to dreams, for if dreams die, life is a broken-winged bird that cannot fly."

In life you are going to meet many dream-killers in passing; the first three dream-killers you are going to encounter will be your parents, your school teachers, and your friends. This is what I call the Three Fs (family, faculty, and friends). Olympic legend Jesse Owens said, "We all have dreams. But in order to make dreams come into reality, it takes an awful lot of determination, dedication, self-discipline, and effort."

Now, don't get me wrong. I'm not saying these people will kill your dreams on purpose; they truly believe they are giving the best advice they can give. When I was in the seventh grade at St. Thomas Parochial School, my teacher told my mother I didn't want to learn. He thought he was being truthful with my mother; my sister Diane and his sister were best friends. But what he didn't know about me was that I had a thirst for knowledge that was unconventional and very artistic. Most teachers back then believed an obedient student was a good student. But the truth is, the student who makes the teacher think more makes the ideal student.

One year later, I attended school on the Lower Eastside of Manhattan. My eighth-grade teacher Mr. Byron helped me to see that all my hopes and dreams could be achieved with faith and hard work. I remember Mr. Byron telling me, "Never bargain your self-respect for someone else's approval." Isn't it funny how one educator can see something in you that other educators couldn't see? That's because Mr. Byron was an artsy person himself and understood me fully. Don't ever let someone steal your dreams from you. Remember: your dreams can come true by working on them. The difference between a dream and a fantasy is that a dream demands action from you; a fantasy won't demand any action at all. Actor Corin Nemec said, "Never let life impede on your ability to manifest your dreams. Dig deeper into your dreams and deeper into yourself and believe that anything is possible, and make it happen."

Surround yourself with the right people, and you can fulfill the dreams. Put yourself in relationships with people who are not only like-minded but also seek to honor God in their own lives. Here is a thought to consider today: if your friends don't point you toward God's goal for you, then they're not very good friends. You want to be surrounded by dream-builders, not dream-killers! When you prune the relationships around you, you're not cutting things out of your life; you're making room for growth so that you can reach your God-given potential. When you make room for God's best, you can walk away from the lesser things that the world has to offer. The key is to keep company only with people who uplift you, whose presence calls forth your best and helps you to manifest your best.

When I was about seventeen years old, I used to hang out at the local radio station WBLS 107.5 in New York City. One of the disc jockeys, Hank Span, took me under his wing as an intern and taught me the ins and outs of broadcast radio. One day I was playing around in the control booth and acting like I was the number-one disc jockey on radio, Frankie Crocker. I was saying the station call letters over and over. Hank Span overheard me and was impressed that I sounded very similar to Frankie Crocker. I will never forget the feeling I had when Hank called radio personality Ken "Spider" Webb over to hear me recite the station call letters. I was feeling overjoyed, excited, and nervous all at the same time. It was my chance to show my talent to the top dogs of radio.

Renowned motivational speaker, author of *The Secret to Success*, activist, and minister Eric Thomas said, "Ask yourself this one question, how bad do you want it?"

So I stepped up to the microphone, and in my best Frankie Crocker–style voice I said, "One-oh-seven point five, WBLS. World's Best-Looking Sound." That day I started my career in radio broadcasting. When it comes to reaching for your goals, you first must dream bigger than anyone can imagine.

Harriet Tubman was an African-American abolitionist, humanitarian, and Union spy during the American Civil War. She said, "Every great dream begins with a dreamer. Always remember, you have within you the strength, the patience, and the passion to reach for the stars to change the world."

Nido Qubein is a businessman, motivational speaker, and the president of High Point University since 2005. He says, "There is no such thing as unrealistic dreams, just unrealistic timelines."

Sometimes you can get caught up in thinking that if you are not making millions of dollars, you won't make a difference. That is simply not true. Most of the great people we read about in history had humble beginnings. They put their plans into action by standing out from the crowd and stepping up to the challenges that were put in front of them. First of all, you must make peace with your mistakes and ask yourself, what is my relationship with the present moment?

Oscar Wilde once said, "A dreamer is one who can only find his way by moonlight, and his punishment is that he sees the dawn before the rest of the world." When you are faced with turmoil, hold those affected in prayer and act as an agent of compassion and understanding. From this day on, take full responsibility for your future. Now is the time to put your dreams in front of your fears. Step into the winner's circle, and claim your prize.

No more standing on the sidelines and waiting for your hero to arrive.

You are the hero you have been waiting for; you are the chosen one. Now is the time to manifest your deepest desires and passionately step out of your comfort zone.

You are uniquely made to do great things in life. God has given you your own DNA (Desire, [K]Nowledge, and Ability) to make your dreams come true. Now embrace your transformation, and accept change in your life.

On this day, you will declare your victory over all of your challenges. Sometimes you may feel like life has thrown you a curveball, but just like an all-star batter, you will hit that ball right out of the park.

Bishop T. D. Jakes once said, "If there's no test, there's no testimony." In life, you have to go through something in order to gain something.

Thank God for the strength to overcome the adversities that life has put you through. Spread your wings and FLY (First Love Yourself).

Remember: there is a solution to every problem. You must focus on the solution and never the problem; that's when the universe will open up to you, and God will guide you through. You are a unique talent, and God has gifted you with the ability to create greatness.

You must recognize your full potential by being grateful to God for your strength. Become the ambassador of peace; practice love, kindness, and patience.

Focus on the peace and presence of God in each person you meet. This is your time to make your prosperity break through.

According to the law of prosperity, you first must have an idea; from that idea, you must take action in order to evolve. Make your mark in the universe, and step forward toward your true self. Give the universe your all, and proclaim your greatness. In the words of motivational speaker Les Brown, "Get out of your own way … You've got something to do!" The time is now.

Marvin Gaye is one of my favorite singers of all time. He recorded the soundtrack for the movie *Trouble Man*. A line in the song says, "There's one thing that I know for sure, and that's taxes, death, and trouble."

In times of trouble, say to yourself, "This too will pass." From this day forward, you will tell the world how you truly feel and share your winnings with the ones you love. Make your mark in this world by showing up and taking on your day to day challenges, while following your dreams. Learning from your mistakes will be your best teacher, but the mistakes you make must be unique to your life's purpose and not someone else's.

"By the time a man realizes that maybe his father was right, he usually has a son who thinks he's wrong." - Charles Wadsworth

Take time to recognize your self-worth and declare the self-love you gratefully deserve. Look at every opportunity as a whisper from God that says, "It is time to show your greatness." Align your heart and mind with God, and awaken the presence of peace, wholeness, abundance, and strength within. Walk in the path that God has blazed for you, and stay focused on your life's mission. Help your loved ones who are in need, and keep your eyes on the prize. Don't give up! And don't settle for less. Make sure you give 100 percent to your mission—play to win. Keep kindness in your heart, and stay in the present moment. It's your time to shine.

Take action!

Notes

CHANGE

Change will not come if we wait for some other person or some other time. We are the ones we've been waiting for. We are the change that we seek.

—Barack Obama

Definition of Change

To make radically different; transform to give a different position, course, or direction to replace with another.

My wife and I have been together for more than twenty-five years now and married for more than twenty-three. And in those twenty-five years we've had our ups and downs, but somehow we have always found a way to work it out. I'm sure she can tell you some stories about me that I sometimes wish had never happened. But since those early years, I've learned to change my mindset and make changes in my behavior so I could help improve our relationship. Zig Ziglar, the author of *See You At the Top* and a motivational speaker, is my inspiration. He helped me to see marriage in a better perspective. He said, "Many marriages would be better if the husband and the wife clearly understood that they are on the same side."

I'm not saying this to make it seem like I was always a deep thinker. The truth is, in the early days of our marriage I often wanted to be right more than I wanted to be happy. Because my wife and I both suffered from what I call "abandonment syndrome," we would at times go at each other over an argument that came from misguided anger. My wife was a child of divorce, and my father died when I was very young, just five years old. We would often take our past anger and fears out on each other. But the best way to overcome your past pains and fears is to recognize them, and then forgive yourself and the person who caused you that pain in the first place. Some couples believe the external attraction they have for one another will meet the internal expectations they want from each other. And those expectations will never meet if you are not willing to make a change in your life. Apple's creator, the genius Steve Jobs said, "For the past thirty-three years, I have looked in the mirror every morning and asked myself: 'If today were the last day of my life, would I want to do what I am about to do today?' And whenever the answer has been 'No' for too many days in a row, I know I need to change something."

The most frightening thing about change is growth. Growth is a very scary place to be when you think you are on your own when it comes to succeeding. The fact of the matter is that if there isn't any change, growth is almost impossible to achieve. The fear of growth goes back to our early childhood. When we were very young, we perceived things at a very fast pace, so when we became adolescents we wanted to make our own decisions without our parents' input. But at the same time, we didn't have the skills to make those life-changing decisions. That's when we start to settle in our ways; that's how change and growth start to pull apart from each other. It's what our elders call "set in your ways." In the words of GE's former CEO Jack Welch, "Change before you have to."

The famous novelist C. S. Lewis gives us a clear understanding of how important change is to our daily lives. He said, "It may be hard for an egg to turn into a bird: it would be a jolly sight harder for it to learn to fly while remaining an egg. We are like eggs at present. And you cannot go on indefinitely being just an ordinary, decent egg. We must be hatched or go bad."

Remember: it is never too late to make changes in your life. My mentor and motivational speaker Dr. Wayne Dyer says, "If you change the way you look at things, the things you look at change."

I remember going to a leadership workshop a few years ago, when author and life coach Brian Tracy said something I'll never forget: "You cannot control what happens to you, but you can control your attitude toward what happens to you, and in that, you will be mastering change rather than allowing it to master you."

Mahatma Gandhi was the preeminent leader of Indian nationalism in British-ruled India, and he said it best: "You must be the change you wish to see in the world."

As Michael Jackson, the world's greatest entertainer, says in a song: "If you want to make the world a better place, you have to look at yourself and make that change."

Law of Attraction guru Natalie Ledwell once told me, "Life is 10 percent of what happens to you, and 90 percent of how you react to it. Often, even in the most challenging situations, you can experience whole new levels of freedom, power, and joy by simply changing the meaning you give something." Most people have a subconscious, self-limiting belief that keeps us from being the true winner that we are. Instead of telling yourself negative things like "If I try, I will fail, and no one will want me," or "I'm not worthy," you have to literally snap yourself out of it. My family and I went through one of the most challenging years of our lives in 2013. You have to evolve from the person you once were into the phenomenal person you truly are. Appreciate the blessings that God has given you; always give it 100 percent. Iyanla Vanzant, life coach and TV host of *Iyanla Fix My Life*, says, "To honor life, we must be willing to grow through what we don't know yet, and outgrow what we know no longer fits us. We must be willing to give in to the process, moment by moment, realizing a new plot may be unfolding."

Many of us think change is a bad thing, but the truth is we will go through some trying times in order to see the light. Sometimes when we are in a state of uncertainty, we will stand still and make excuses about why it can't be done, but it's going to take all of you to change from the old you into the person God intended. Stepping into your truth is the next step you must take in order to live in the present moment. You must constantly transform your life in order to be competitive in today's job market or in your business. Transformation is the key to growth. For example: Dunkin Donuts was just a donut shop in the '70s and '80s; their ad announced, "Time to make the donuts." Because of the competition of Starbucks and other coffee shops across the country, now Dunkin Donuts' motto is "Fresh coffee every day." Without making that change and transforming from a donut shop to a coffeehouse, Dunkin Donuts may have gone under in the midst of the recession.

Most people won't make changes in their life until the pain of remaining the same becomes greater than the pain of changing. Remember: change is always opportunity. It is the time to overcome your adversities and stand committed to the spirit of good.

Focus on the presence of God and find that life unfolds with ease and grace. You must do the things today that others will not do, so that you can have the things tomorrow that others will not have. Thank God for all of your talents, gifts, and abilities to help you overcome conflicts that may arise in your daily encounters.

Motivational speaker and mentor Lisa Nichols once said, "The longest journey you will take in life will be from your head to your heart."

This Too Will Pass (Life Is What You Make It)

My mother once told me that when she a young girl and things wouldn't work out or go her way, my grandmother would sit her down and tell her the story of her hand. She would say, "The fingers on your hand come in many sizes. Life is a lot like your fingers. Some are longer than others; just like your fingers, life has its ups and downs."

The best teacher you will ever encounter will be life experiences. There will be times in your life when you will feel like throwing both hands in the air and calling it quits. George Bernard Shaw, Irish playwright and a cofounder of the London School of Economics, said, "A life spent making mistakes is not only more honorable, but more useful than a life spent doing nothing."

When my wife was diagnosed with breast cancer, I felt like getting on my knees and crying for the whole day. My wife is such a strong woman. Just feeling her positive energy gave me more courage than I could imagine. I remember seeing a sign that had a quote by Russian physician, dramaturge, and author Anton Chekhov, who is considered to be among the greatest writers of short stories in history. It said, "Any idiot can face a crisis—it's day-to-day living that wears you out."

Just think about that statement for a moment. If you are already taking on the day-to-day challenges that life hits you with, then surely you have the strength to take on any crisis that may come your way. Henry David Thoreau said, "I went to the woods because I wished to live deliberately, to confront only the essential facts of life, and see if I could not learn what it had to teach, and not, when I came to die, discover that I had not lived."

When life seems to be a constant struggle, it's because you are not on the path that God intended for you. When you face challenges in life, you are on the right path because you're given tools to overcome those challenges and make headway. A challenge is meant to strengthen, teach, and mature you.

Monica Palmer, entertainment executive and manager of R&B singer Johnny Gill, once told me, "Constantly struggling means you're going against the current and will be worn down. Are you struggling or facing challenges? Discover your purpose, and understand the difference."

A scripture comes to mind when I think about life's challenges that we have to overcome.

So many enemies against one Man all of them trying to kill me. To them I'm just a broken-down wall or a tottering fence. They plan to topple me from my high position.

They delight in telling lies about me. They are friendly to my face, but they curse me in their hearts. I wait quietly before God for my hope is in him. He alone is my rock and my salvation, my fortress where I will not be shaken.

My salvation and my honor came from God alone. He is my refuge, a rock where no enemy can reach me. O my people trust in him at all times pour out your heart to him for God is our refuge. From the greatest to the lowliest—all are nothing in his sight.

If you weigh them on the scales, they are lighter than a puff of air. Don't try to get rich by extortion or robbery.

And if your wealth increases, don't make it the center of your life. God has spoken plainly, and I have heard it many times; unfailing love, O Lord, is yours. Surely you judge all people according to what they have done. (Psalm 62)

I mention this because at times we stop moving forward in life and think dwelling on the past will somehow make things better. In fact, it will have an opposite effect on the situation. That scripture simply tells us to hold on to God's grace and believe that no matter what, he will see you through. The Honorable Bob Marley was a Jamaican singer-songwriter and musician best known for his reggae records. He once said, "Open your eyes, look within. Are you satisfied with the life you're living?"

I once read a Facebook post that said, "When you have no strength left, you have no choice but to rely on the strength of a saner Power to restore you to Wholeness. In the pursuit of our souls, Spirit takes no prisoners."

He who overcomes others is strong; he who overcomes himself is mighty. Today is the day you recognize your joy and live up to your life's expectations.

Make your dream come true by visualizing yourself as the winner you were created to be. Set a GOAL (Get Out and Live), and put your plan into action.

Ask yourself, what's holding me back? My mentor and motivational speaker Les Brown once said, "There are winners, there are losers and there are people who have not discovered how to win." Now is the time to discover your way to win. Start out your day by saying to yourself, "Through God, all things are possible. I'm blessed and highly favored." Start to look at your life through mindsight, not just eyesight.

Make your mind up that you will win. Don't talk about the negative things that happen to you—that will just attract more negativity.

Focus on the solution. Understand that it's possible to have your dream come true, and it's necessary to make it a reality. Ask yourself, am I evading my own greatness? You are the captain of your ship. So sail on!

This is the time to embrace your transformation and accept change in your life. Take time out today to observe the beautiful world that surrounds you. Accept grace with a grateful heart. Have patience, and hear the music, feel the wind blow, get connected with the true you. Ask yourself this question: what are some of the biggest challenges I've had to overcome in my life? Some of them may feel like they happened yesterday, this morning, or maybe this moment. But if you take the time to feel the presence of God and think about some of the challenges that you have already overcome, that's when the doors of opportunity will open up and help you transform your life.

Every great dream begins with a dreamer. Always remember, you have within you the strength, the patience, and the passion to reach for the stars to change the world.

—Harriet Tubman

So make that change.

Notes

TRUTH

When you do the common things in life in an
uncommon way, you will command the attention
of the world.

—George Washington Carver

Definition of Truth

*The state of being the case; fact; the body of real things, events, and facts;
actuality often capitalized; a transcendent fundamental or spiritual
reality; a judgment, proposition, or idea that is true or accepted as truth;
the body of true statements and propositions.*

When I was about nine years old, my mother had me take piano
lessons. Every other day after school, I had to go across the street
from my home to Miss Mill's second-floor apartment to learn the
piano. Back then I thought anything that took me away from playing
outside or watching my favorite cartoons was just pure cruelty. But
what I didn't know back then was that my mother wanted me to see
things from a broader spectrum. She would say, "A scared man can't
gamble, and a jealous man can't work."

Learning the piano was my introduction to finding my way
in this world. My mother wanted to give me the opportunity she
didn't have to express herself. Now, let me tell you a little bit about
my mother. She was nicknamed by her friends as the Sarge. My

mother is what most people would call a pure leader; even in spirit, my mother is the glue that holds our family together. I am the youngest of six, and growing up as the baby of a big family had its up and downs. I say this because I couldn't do some of the things my older siblings did, because Mom had already checked them on it. At the same time, she would give me things that my sibs didn't get. Growing up in the Big Apple was a plus for me because I was, and still am, a very "artsy" person.

As I got older, music took over my life, and I began to look at the world as one big music note. I told my mother I wanted to play the trumpet, so she bought me a trumpet and had me take lessons from one of the members of the jazz trio Dayton Selby. Shortly after that, I started taking drum lessons. By the time I was fifteen, I was playing six different musical instruments (three of them I taught myself to play), and found my truth in the world. Or so I thought ...

At that time, a new brand of music was taking over the streets of New York City. We called it hip-hop. I used to go to afterschool parties (back then we called them jams) at a place named Mr. Souls. It was there that I fell in love with DJing. I watched DJs like DJ AJ, DJ Hollywood, DJ Lovebug Starski, and Grandmaster Flash do what they do best.

I didn't go to Mr. Souls for the DJs. I went for the music, because I was also a break dancer. (We were called B boys back then). One night I watched Lovebug Starski DJing, and I was hooked! He played a record called "Dance to the Drummer's Beat" and then "Dance with Me." He must have played those two records for a half hour. I stopped dancing and watched him mix and get the crowd jumping. On that day, I made up my mind to become a DJ. For weeks I asked my mother to buy me DJ equipment so I could get started on my new career. At first, my mother was a little hesitant about buying me the equipment, but in the word of entrepreneur and motivational speaker Jim Rohn, "The worst thing one can do is not to try, to be aware of what one wants and not give in to it, to spend years in silent hurt wondering if something could have materialized—never knowing."

So I asked my Aunt Weez and eldest sister Diane if they could buy the equipment. For weeks I pestered many family members, until my mother bought me a stereo unit. And the unit was top of the line; it had all the bells and whistles. I started my new path in music, practicing the best way I knew how by watching DJs in the park and at the schoolyard jams. Then I would go home and do exactly what I saw them do.

I then recruited my nephew Darrell and my two best buddies from high school, Andre and Derek, and my neighbor David, who lived downstairs, as my emcees, a.k.a. rappers. I was on my way to becoming a star ... or so I thought.

When I was a junior at Benjamin Franklin High School, my friends and I would give school parties to get attention from girls and to make some money. At that time hip-hop was very young, and I took advantage of every opportunity that came my way. Randy Sanders, a.k.a. DJ Randy D of the Harlem World Crew, took me under his wing and taught me the business, from promotion to marketing. I also made my way as a DJ-slash-club promoter in some of the top clubs, retail record shops, radio stations, and indie record companies in New York City, like Harlem World, The Rooftop, Downtown Records, Downstairs Records, 107.5 WBLS, and Select Records, just to name a few. As years went on, I worked my way up the music-business ladder; I started my own record company and opened a recording studio, and I worked with dozens of recording artists in the music business. In the words of the late great Ray Charles, "I was born with music inside me. Music was one of my parts. Like my ribs, my kidneys, my liver, my heart. Like my blood. It was a force already within me when I arrived on the scene. It was a necessity for me, like food or water."

Those early years in the world of hip-hop gave me the tools that I use today in my businesses. Confucius said, "Choose a job you love, and you will never have to work a day in your life." The truth is, when you have that burning desire, that thing that calls you, don't run from it—run to it. This is how you know it's your true calling. What do family and friends come to you for, and how do they view you? Ask yourself these three questions:

(1) What do I like to do?
(2) What would I do for free?
(3) What comes easy to me that is hard for others?

If you answer these questions truthfully, no matter who or what tries to stand in your way, you will prosper and overcome all obstacles. In the words of a true champion, boxing legend Muhammad Ali, "I know where I'm going and I know the truth, and I don't have to be what you want me to be. I'm free to be what I want."

The time is now to give 100 percent of yourself to your true calling. My mother would often tell me, "Life stands still for no man."

Once you put God first and look deep inside yourself, the universe will serve you what your heart truly desires. Life coach and mentor Lisa Nichols once told me, "You are the designer of your destiny; you are the author of your story."

Just a few years ago, my wife and I started a business in real estate. We wanted to earn more capital so our children would have more money for college. So we signed up for classes in real estate investing (REI). The training and events were very exciting and fast-paced, and we thought that was the direction we were supposed to take; but after two and a half years into that fast-paced life, things started to slow down. And then superstorm Sandy hit New York with a vengeance. American author, advertising executive, and politician Bruce Barton once said, "Nothing splendid has ever been achieved except by those who dared believe that something inside them was superior to circumstance."

Soon after the storm, deals weren't as lucrative, and money stopped coming in. The bills were piling up. We began to take additional loans just to pay our day-to-day bills. It's hard to even think straight when bill collectors are ringing your phone off the hook. Understand this; you are not a victim of circumstance. You are the powerful creator of your experience and your destiny. Spiritual guide and minister Dr. Deepak Chopra said, "Always go with your passions. Never ask yourself if it's realistic or not."

I know from experience that digging down deep in your soul for your truth puts you in a painful and scary place that can sometimes make you feel lonely inside when you make that change in your life. But you must go to that dark and scary place in order to become free. Former South African President Nelson Mandela once said, "Does anybody really think that they didn't get what they had because they didn't have the talent or the strength or the endurance or the commitment?"

In order to carry out a positive action, we must develop a positive vision of ourselves. Create a vision board of your life for the best you possible. See yourself in the now as a better you. Step into your truth, and create a new pathway for your future. Buddha once said, "There are only two mistakes one can make along the road to truth; not going all the way, and not starting."

Always concentrate on the solution, never the problem. And the truth shall make you free.

> For every good reason there is to lie, there is a better reason to tell the truth.
> —Robert "Bo" Bennett

The Present Moment (Make Every Moment Count)

On this day you will stand out from the crowd, put together your life plan, and make a major difference in the world. This is the time you wise up and make your to-do list and you're not-to-do list. You are invincible and fearless. Step up to the challenge that's in front of you, and make peace with your mistakes. When you are faced with turmoil, hold those affected in prayer, and act as an agent of compassion and understanding.

Ask yourself, what is my relationship with the present moment? And from this day on, take responsibility for your future. Now is the time to put your dreams in front of your fears. Step into the winner's circle and claim your prize.

From the time you wake up in the morning to start your day, you should be living in the present moment. What I mean when I say "the present moment" is the mindset of now. For example: when you wake up in the morning and jump in the shower, your concentration should be on taking that shower and nothing else. When eating breakfast, your mind is only on eating breakfast.

If you start thinking about how your day will go, your mind will start driving to work before you do and begin your workday before you do. When you set out to start your workday, traffic will become frustrating, and you will be anxious the whole trip in to work; by the time you get there, because you also thought about your work duties you're tired and ready to go home an hour into work.

Buddha once said, "Do not dwell in the past; do not dream of the future, concentrate the mind on the present moment."

Emmet Fox was a New Thought spiritual leader of the early twentieth century, famous for his large Divine Science church services held in New York City during the Great Depression. He said, "The art of life is to live in the present moment, and to make that moment as perfect as we can by the realization that we are the instruments and expression of God Himself."

Thích Nhất Hạnh is a Vietnamese Zen Buddhist monk, teacher, author, poet, and peace activist. He lives in the Plum Village Monastery in the Dordogne region in the south of France who travels internationally to give retreats and talks. He says, "Hope is important because it can make the present moment less difficult to bear. If we believe that tomorrow will be better, we can bear a hardship today."

The one question you must ask yourself every day is, what is my relationship with the present moment? The importance of staying in the present moment is so you can concentrate on your creative side. Doing that will help you overcome your past and prepare you for your future.

Sharon Salzberg is a *New York Times* bestselling author and influential teacher of Buddhist meditation practices in the West. In 1974, she cofounded the Insight Meditation Society at Barre, Massachusetts, with Jack Kornfield and Joseph Goldstein. She said, "We can have skills training in mindfulness so that we are using our attention to perceive something in the present moment. This perception is not so latent by fears or projections into the future, or old habits, and then I can actually stir loving-kindness or compassion in skills training too, which can be sort of provocative, I found."

The other question you must ask yourself is, what mattered to me five years ago, and does it matter to me now? Sometimes we find ourselves dwelling in the past, never giving the present a chance to manifest. In order for your future to manifest joy, you have to stand in your truth and let go of the past demons that keep you from moving forward.

Chanakya was an Indian teacher, philosopher, and royal advisor. He is also considered one of the world's first political scientists and economists. He is referred to as the Father of Economics. He said, "We should not fret for what is past, nor should we be anxious about the future; men of discernment deal only with the present moment."

Take responsibility for your future. Now is the time to put your dreams in front of your fears. Step into the winner's circle, and claim your prize.

> There is no better than adversity. Every defeat, every heartbreak, every loss, contains its own seed, its own lesson on how to improve your performance the next time.
>
> —Malcolm X

Stand in your truth.

Notes

SERVICE

Service to others is the rent you pay for your room
here on earth.

—Muhammad Ali

Definition of Service

*The occupation or function of serving- Employment as a servant.
The work performed by one that serves; Help; use; benefit (glad to be of
service); contribution to the welfare of others.*

I've told you a little bit about my mother. Now let me tell you
a bit about my father. He was the middle child of three, with an
older sister and a younger sister. My father grew up in Detroit,
Michigan, during the Great Depression. He also served in the armed
forces in World War II and fought at the battle of St. Anna in
Italy. After an honorable discharge as an army sergeant, he enrolled
at Northwestern University in Chicago as a business major. After
graduating from NWU, he worked for Chrysler for a number of
years. When I think about my father, I often think about what the
US representative for Illinois's third congressional district once said:
"On this Veterans Day, let us remember the service of our veterans,
and let us renew our national promise to fulfill our sacred obligations
to our veterans and their families who have sacrificed so much so
that we can live free."

From the time I was a little boy, I've always looked at life differently than my peers. I remember the day I got lost in the hospital; my father was looking all over for me. The nurses kept me with them at the nurses' station. I remember my father walking up with a happy and relieved look on his face as he said to me, "Hey! Man, where have you been? I've been looking all over the hospital for you. I thought you ran off, man."

The nurses were in shock that this grown man was talking to a little boy that way. One nurse asked, "Who are these people? And who is this man, talking to this baby like that?"

Before anyone could answer, I said, "That's my sister Blenda (Brenda), and that's my Daddy-O!"

I tell that story because my father and I had a very special relationship. Even though my father left this earth in the physical form, he has still been with me all through my life. I'm not saying this to make you think I'm some overly religious person. In fact, I'm not. The Dalai Lama explained it best: "This is my simple religion. There is no need for temples; no need for complicated philosophy. Our own brain, our own heart is our temple; the philosophy is kindness."

The most important thing about service is paying it forward, not giving back. Once you have searched your soul for your true calling, serving God is the next step in following your dreams and aspirations. Mahatma Gandhi once said, "The best way to find you is to lose yourself in the service of others."

When I look at my children and see so much hope and ambition in their eyes, that's all the motivation I need to keep going. I sometimes look back on my life and say to myself, "You are truly blessed with family and love. Thank you, God."

Just thinking about the sacrifices that my wife and I make when it comes to our children is sometimes mind-blowing. But at the same time, it's very fulfilling. Pastor Charles Stanley puts it profoundly: "In giving us children, God places us in a position of both leadership and service. He calls us to give up our lives for someone else's sake—to abandon our own desires and put our child's interests first. Yet, according to His perfect design, it is through this selflessness that we can become truly fulfilled."

I'm not saying this because I feel you should give up on your dreams or your children's dreams. But the dream of having a family and raising kids carries numerous responsibilities and requires huge sacrifices. In the words of Russian-American novelist and philosopher Ayn Rand, "It only stands to reason that where there's sacrifice, there's someone collecting the sacrificial offerings. Where there's service, there is someone being served. The man who speaks to you of sacrifice is speaking of slaves and masters, and intends to be the master."

Some religious philosophers say you can't serve two masters. But I say that is exactly what God's grace is telling us to do. If you master the true calling that God has designed for you, which is service to God and mankind, then that service is the victory we seek in our daily lives.

> Show me your hands. Do they have scars from giving? Show me your feet. Are they wounded in service? Show me your heart. Have you left a place for divine love?
>
> —Fulton J. Sheen

Earl Nightingale was an American motivational speaker and author known as the Dean of Personal Development. He was the voice of Sky King, the hero of a radio adventure series in the early 1950s, and a WGN radio show host from 1950 to 1956. I used to listen to his tapes when I was a teenager. His words made me feel like I could conquer the world. One thing that he said sticks with me to this day: "We will receive not what we idly wish for but what we justly earn. Our rewards will always be in exact proportion to our service."

Most people think that when they are telling others what to do, that means that they are in command; in reality, you are only in command of yourself. I used to suffer from what I call "I know what's best for you" syndrome. I thought telling others how to live their lives was my way of giving service to God, but the real reason I was always giving my opinion to others was because I didn't want to face my own shortcomings. I know now that the only way to serve others is to serve you first. After fixing you first, you can then help someone else. James Allen was a British philosophical writer known for his inspirational books and poetry and as a pioneer of the self-help movement. His best-known work is *As a Man Thinketh*. He said, "A man has to learn that he cannot command things, but that he can command himself; that he cannot coerce the wills of others, but that he can mold and master his own will: and things serve him who serves Truth; people seek guidance of him who is master of himself."

In your deepest, darkest moment, it's up to you to give the universe your best. I know that is easier said than done.

Most people think the wealthy got their riches the easy way, but the truth is, the majority of the wealthiest people on the planet came from poverty. No matter what you want to do in life, give it 100 percent. Service is the opposite of selfishness. When you put your wants before your, or anyone else's, needs, that is selfishness. Always put needs before wants. Actress Gillian Anderson said, "Be of service. Whether you make yourself available to a friend or coworker, or you make time every month to do volunteer work, there is nothing that harvests more of a feeling of empowerment than being of service to someone in need."

I've learned in that in order for you to serve God with all your heart and soul, you first must learn to serve yourself with all of your heart and soul.

What I know for sure is this: God is love. And his philosophy is kindness. So when I say you must serve yourself first, I mean you must be of service to your fellow man. That's what God intended us to do. No one becomes successful on his or her own. All of the most successful people on this planet have a success team with them. Louise Hay is an American motivational author and the founder of Hay House. She has authored several New Thought self-help books and is best known for her 1984 book, *You Can Heal Your Life*. She says, "I find that when we really love and accept and approve of ourselves exactly as we are, then everything in life works."

In life there are givers and there are takers. The question to ask yourself is, which one am I? If you give for the sake of giving and no other reason, you are a giver.

Dr. Maya Angelou says, "If you have only one smile in you, give it to the people you love."

Give as God gives, with no expectations of receiving anything in return. Serving God will give you the strength you need to service your fellow man and make a difference.

Take this time to look inside yourself and become a rising star; give the universe something to talk about. Too many times, you have talked yourself out of your greatness by looking at your past mistakes and saying to yourself, "No need to try. I will just fail anyway."

John F. Kennedy once said, "Those who dare to fail miserably can achieve greatly." Stepping out of your comfort zone is a way to build your consciousness and help you become stronger. It's time to MAP (Mental Action Plan) out a direction you want to go toward and then put it into action. Dream big; set a power goal.

Move your goalpost and excite your imagination with a direct, major power plan. People who create power goals live on purpose and know what they are up to in life. Don't just look up to your heroes; look into your heroes. You will see they are just like you, only fearless. Get out of your own way, and unleash the true you.

> Whatever we plant in our subconscious mind and nourish with repetition and emotion will one day become a reality.
>
> —Earl Nightingale

Understanding (When You Know Better, You Do Better)

When we understand God's designed path for us, we can move toward his kingdom of joy. In the Faith chapter, I told you about going to see the play *The Wiz*, a spin-off of *The Wizard of Oz*. The play later became a movie starring Diana Ross and Michael Jackson. What I love about this story is that you can see yourself as the main character. The story is much like life experiences. You will go through lots of ups and downs, hit a few bumps in the road, and meet a host of characters on your journey to find the real you. Nelson Mandela once said, "I learned that courage was not the absence of fear, but the triumph over it. The brave man is not he who does not feel afraid, but he who conquers that fear."

I remember having a conversation with a former coworker on the subjects of racism and sexism. One of our coworkers was complaining about another coworker. "He thinks he's black." I asked, "Why do you feel that way?" Before she could answer, another coworker jumped in and said, "She feels that way because he is married to a black woman, and his kids are black."

As the conversation progressed, I wondered what in his behavior had warranted such an accusation. What I learned from that conversation is that when it comes to subjects like racism or sexism, most people will speak with a sense of tolerance, not from understanding. Let me explain the difference between the two. Tolerance has a limit, a boiling point. We are taught to tolerate each other's race, religion, and lifestyle, but when you simply tolerate the differences between people without understanding, you are setting yourself up for disappointment. Dr. Martin Luther King Jr. once said, "Shallow understanding from people of good will is more frustrating than absolute misunderstanding from people of ill will." When we have absolute understanding of one another, no matter what, respect will take over and compassion will overcome any differences we may have of one another." In fact, anger and intolerance are the enemies of correct understanding. True understanding forms a deeper connection to your soul then tolerance.

Oprah Winfrey once said, "It isn't until you come to a spiritual understanding of who you are—not necessarily a religious feeling, but deep down, the spirit within—that you can begin to take control."

Having an authentic understanding of yourself will help you understand your neighbor and his or her culture, religion, or beliefs. Confucius said, "I hear and I forget. I see and I remember. I do and I understand."

You are invincible and fearless. Step up to the challenge that's in front of you, and make peace with your mistakes. When you are faced with turmoil, hold those affected in prayer and act as an agent of compassion and understanding. Albert Einstein said, "Peace cannot be kept by force; it can only be achieved by understanding."

Bishop T. D. Jakes said, "Give a man a fish; you'll feed him for a day. Teach a man how to fish; he will eat for a lifetime. Show a man how to buy the pond, and no one in his family will know struggle."

Today you will stand up and show out and make this day the day you claim your greatness. This is what I know for sure: pain is inevitable, and suffering is a choice. Don't let someone or something steal your joy. If you allow God to guide you through your troubling times, things will work out. Franklin D. Roosevelt once said, "Happiness lies in the joy of achievement and the thrill of creative effort." Stick to what truly makes you happy. Be passionate about your "why." Surround yourself with like-minded souls. In the words of Mother Teresa, "Joy is prayer; joy is strength; joy is love; joy is a net of love by which you can catch souls." Make this day and every day your day of joy. Have a blessed day, and pay it forward.

Be of service by doing a service.

Notes

Printed in the United States
By Bookmasters